Written by
Alem Aweke

Illustrated by
Yorris Handoko

Illustrated by Yorris Handoko

Hardcover ISBN: 978-1-959202-10-3
Paperback ISBN: 978-1-959202-11-0

Library of Congress Control Number: 2025919627

Lella Menged LLC
5900 Balcones Drive
Suite 100
Austin, TX 78731

www.lella-menged.com

For the brave Ethiopians who stood together and fell at Adwa.

Acknowledgments

I want to thank all of you who have contributed to this children's book in one way or another. I am especially grateful to Tesfaye Aragie, Fesseha Atlaw, Biniam Habtewold, Bereket Aweke, Biniam Hirut, and Kesis Henok Tezera for their support in providing materials, thoughtful reviews, and valuable recommendations.

I am deeply appreciative of the outstanding editorial work by Krista Zimonick, whose expertise greatly enhanced this book. I would also like to extend my heartfelt gratitude to my wife and daughter, whose love, encouragement, and patience gave me the strength and inspiration to bring this project to life.

The Race for Africa

A long time ago, in the 1880s and 1890s, Europe was buzzing with big machines and noisy factories. But to keep those machines running, the Europeans needed shiny gold, rubber, and oil, and they knew where to find them: in Africa!

So, many European countries hurried to Africa to grab land and treasures. They wanted to get rich! This race was called the Scramble for Africa.

The leaders from countries such as Belgium, France, Germany, Britain, and Italy held a big meeting called the Berlin Conference. But guess what? They didn't invite any African leaders! They made plans to divide Africa without asking the people who lived there.

The Wuchale Treaty

Italy wanted to be a big and powerful country too. So, it looked toward Ethiopia, a strong and free land.

In May 1889, Italy and Ethiopia made a special promise called the Wuchale Treaty. Emperor Menelik II signed it, hoping it would keep the peace. But Empress Taytu didn't trust it. Something about it just didn't feel right …

A Tricky Promise

And, uh-oh! There was a big mistake in the treaty! Article 17, one of the rules, said different things in each country's language. In Italian, it said that Ethiopia had to talk to other countries *only* through Italy. But in Amharic, Ethiopia's language, it said Ethiopia *could* talk to other countries through Italy if *it wanted to*.

Empress Taytu was right to be suspicious! That tiny mix-up caused huge trouble later on.

When Emperor Menelik found out what the Italian version of the treaty said, he was very upset. He wrote a letter to King Umberto of Italy to complain. But the king didn't care.

Some powerful countries such as Britain and Germany took Italy's side. Britain even said it would be better if Italy ruled Ethiopia! Germany refused to sell Ethiopia any weapons. But France and Russia stood with Ethiopia and wanted to help.

The Brave Empress

Later, Italy sent Count Antonelli, the man who wrote the treaty, to talk to the Emperor.

Count Antonelli stood tall and said, "Italy will never say the treaty is wrong. We are a powerful country and will protect our pride, even with our army!"

Empress Taytu was angry but brave. She said, "I may be a woman, and I don't like war, but I would rather *die* than accept your unfair deal. We will never give up our home. Dying for our country is an honor!"

The March Toward War

Italy sent a man named Baratieri to lead the mission. He had a tricky idea: if he could get Ethiopia's local kings to argue, maybe Italy could take over more easily.

Ethiopia had many regions, each with its own leader. Sometimes they disagreed, but when danger came, they stood strong together!

In December 1894, General Baratieri brought nine thousand soldiers and marched toward the town of Adwa. Among his troops were Askari, African soldiers recruited from neighboring regions, as well as Ethiopians who had been hired to help.

On March 3, 1895, the Italians captured the town of Adigrat.

But Emperor Menelik didn't rush into battle. The Italians thought he was scared or weak, but they were very wrong. While they waited, Menelik was quietly preparing his army to defend Ethiopia!

Adigrat

Ethiopia

The Call to Defend the Land

On September 17, 1895, Emperor Menelik sent an important message to the people of Ethiopia.

He said, "An enemy has come to take our land and hurt our faith. I tried to keep peace, but they won't stop. Now, with God's help, I will protect what our ancestors gave us. If you can fight, come with me. If not, please pray for us."

Ethiopia didn't have one big army like some other countries. But it had something just as powerful: a proud tradition of fearless warriors.

From all over the country, people came together. They spoke different languages and had different beliefs, but they all came together. Christians and Muslims stood side by side to defend their homeland.

Women prepared food like injera to nourish the soldiers. Able men grabbed their weapons, and women stood beside them, ready too.

Marching for Ethiopia

Emperor Menelik began marching north from Addis Ababa with his army. He told the southern soldiers to meet at a place called Warra Ilu, and others were asked to join him at Mekele.

As they marched, the sound of drums, horns, and songs filled the air. Singers joked, "Wow! They came all the way across the sea to take Abyssinia!" Everyone was coming together to protect their home.

Empress Taytu brought thousands of brave soldiers too. But her group also included ladies from the court and over 100 musicians playing the kirar, a traditional eight-stringed instrument. Their music made the long march lively and joyful.

By the time they reached Tigray, the Ethiopian army had grown to more than 100,000 strong! They came from many regions.

Many others came with spears and swords, ready to defend Ethiopia!

Emperor Menelik called upon leaders such as King Kawo Tona of Wolaita, King Abba Jifar II of Jimma, and others to help secure and unify the rest of the country.

Ethiopian Forces

Emperor Menelik II

Riflemen
30,000
Cavalry
12,000
Cannons
32

Empress Taytu

Riflemen
3,000
Cavalry
6,000

Ras Wele

Riflemen
10,000

Ras Mikael

Riflemen
6,000
Cavalry
10,000

Ras Makonnen

Riflemen
15,000

Ras Mengesha Atikem

Riflemen
6,000

Ras Mengesha Yohannes and Ras Alula

Riflemen
15,000

King Tekle Haymanot

Riflemen
5,000

Militias with swords, shields and spears: 20,000

Italian Forces

Meanwhile, Italy's army, led by General Baratieri, had about 15,000 soldiers split into four groups:

- The Right Column, led by General Dabormida

- The Center Column, led by General Arimondi

- The Left Column, made of Askaris (African soldiers), led by General Albertone

- The Reserve Column, led by General Ellena

Even though Italy had modern weapons and trained soldiers, there were much fewer of them than the huge force of united Ethiopian warriors!

Italian Forces

General Baratieri

Left Column	Center Column	Right Column
General Albertone	**General Arimondi**	**General Dabormida**

Riflemen **4,300**	Riflemen **3,300**	Riflemen **4,800**
Cannons **14**	Cannons **12**	Cannons **18**

Reserve Column

General Ellena

Riflemen **3,000**

Cannons **12**

The First Victory

At a tall hill called Amba Alage, Italian soldiers were watching from above. Their leader, Major Pietro Toselli, was under General Arimondi. One day in December 1895, they looked down, and couldn't believe their eyes!

Ras Makonnen was coming through the mountains with 40,000 Ethiopian soldiers. Toselli shouted, "Sono molti, molti!" That means, "They are many, many!" in Italian. And guess what? That was just the front of the army; more were still coming!

Ras Makonnen, Fitawrari Gebeyehu, and Ras Mengesha Yohannes commanded the Ethiopian soldiers. Early in the morning, a small group of soldiers distracted the Italians. Then, from other sides, Ras Wele, Ras Mangasha, and Ras Alula led powerful attacks!

Ethiopian soldiers climbed the steep hills with bravery. The Italian army got scared and started to run. Some even rolled their big cannons down the hill so they wouldn't be taken!

By afternoon, the hill of Amba Alage was the site of Ethiopia's victory.

That night, one of Ras Mangasha's soldiers ran more than 50 miles to bring the news to the rest of the army.

Breathing hard, he said, "The Italian army is beaten! We got their cannons and rifles!"

Brave and Clever at Mekele

About 35 miles from Amba Alage, the Italians had built a strong stone fort in a town called Mekele. Its thick walls made it hard for cannonballs to break through. Inside, Major Galliano was in charge, along with Italian and Askari soldiers.

In January 1896, Ras Makonnen and his troops surrounded the fort. Soon after, Emperor Menelik arrived and set up his big red tent nearby. The soldiers whispered, "It's the Negus!", which means the "King"!

The very next day, Empress Taytu sent food, cows, sheep, and butter to feed the Ethiopian soldiers. She was ready to wait and win.

The Ethiopians fired their cannons all day, but the fort stayed strong. From the right and left, Bejirond Balcha, later known as Dejazmach Balcha, and Likemekuas Abate bravely directed their cannons. Then Taytu noticed something important. The Italian soldiers were getting water from two nearby springs. So, she came up with a smart plan: take the springs!

Her plan worked! Ethiopian soldiers quietly took over the water. Now the Italians had no clean water, and they grew tired and thirsty.

Soon, Italy sent someone to ask for peace. Emperor Menelik agreed to let the Italians go, but only if they gave up the fort without a fight.

On January 20, the Italians waved a white flag! They even paid for animals to help carry their things as they left. And as they marched away, the red, yellow, and green flags of Ethiopia flew proudly over Mekele!

A Spy with a Secret

After marching north to a place called Gundapta, near Adwa, Emperor Menelik hoped to prevent more fighting. He asked Italy to talk about peace. But General Baratieri said no. He wanted Ethiopia to agree to Italy's version of the Wuchale Treaty, which gave Italy control. He also wanted to keep the land Italy had taken.

The Italians built a strong fort at Adigrat, hoping Menelik would attack there. But Emperor Menelik was too smart! Instead of going to Adigrat, he moved his army around it, cutting off Italy's supplies and messages.

On February 22, Menelik moved his troops even closer to Adwa. A week later, General Baratieri met with his four generals: Albertone, Arimondi, Dabormida, and Ellena. He said he'd wait to hear from his spies before deciding what to do.

But one of his spies who was an Ethiopian, Basha Awalom, was really helping the Ethiopians! The Italians didn't know. He tricked them by saying Menelik's army was falling apart and some kings had left. Baratieri believed the lie.

That night, the Italian army began quietly marching toward Adwa, hoping to sneak up on the Ethiopians in the dark. But one group, led by Major Turitto, got too close, and Ras Alula's scouts spotted them!

The Church Vigil

At 4 o'clock in the morning on March 1, Emperor Menelik and Empress Taytu were at church, praying very quietly. Suddenly, a messenger ran in with big news, the Italian army was coming!

Menelik finished the prayer calmly and got ready for the big battle.

Menelik always brought the Tabot of St. George when he went to war. In the Ethiopian Orthodox Church, a Tabot is a holy object that stands for the Ark of the Covenant. Each one is dedicated to a saint, like St. George.

Guess what? March 1 was St. George's feast day, a lucky day to fight! Priests from the city of Axum also carried the Tabot of St. Mary to bless and help the army.

The Battle of Adwa

The Italian soldiers bumped into Ras Mangasha's men by accident! Empress Taytu, with 5,000 brave soldiers led by Balcha, rushed to help. King Tekle Haimanot came with 4,000 to 5,000 soldiers, and Ras Wele brought 10,000 more. Emperor Menelik's big army of 35,000 waited in the valley. The Italians were surrounded and outnumbered; they had walked right into a trap!

Major Turitto's group had marched too far ahead and lost touch with the rest of the Italians. They couldn't get help or run away. Albertone's soldiers set up about a mile behind, thinking they were safe between two mountains.

When the sun came up, Menelik lined up his troops to face Albertone's army. This was the open battle Menelik wanted, not a hidden fight like before.

No one knew it yet, but this battle wasn't just for Ethiopia, it was a fight for the whole future of Africa!

The Ethiopian soldiers charged the middle of the Italian line. Menelik's special guards ran down the hill, but the Italians pushed them back at first. Then Empress Taytu shouted bravely, lifted her veil, and said, "What's going on? Be brave! Victory is ours!" Her courage made all the soldiers cheer. Even more women joined her, lifting everyone's spirits.

Meanwhile, the pieces of the battle were falling into place. Menelik cheered on the cannon crews. Ras Makonnen and Ras Mikael came in from one side, and Tekle Haimanot and Empress Taytu led soldiers from the other side, trapping the Italians!

Baratieri told General Dabormida to help Albertone, but Dabormida got lost at a fork in the road. The Ethiopians took advantage fast! They sent 15,000 soldiers, led by Ras Makonnen and Ras Mangasha, right between the two Italian groups, cutting them off from each other.

The Italians were Routed!

At first, the Italian Askari soldiers started to run away.
The Ethiopians, full of energy and pride, charged forward,
drumming and cheering loudly under waving Ethiopian flags.

The Italians felt scared and sad. General Albertone was hurt and
trapped; he had to give up. His capture was one of the biggest
wins of the day!

Baratieri told his soldiers to run away, but it was too late. From
the high hills, Ras Alula, Ras Mangasha, Ras Mikael, and the
fearless Oromo horse riders were rushing in fast!

The Oromo riders wore wild lions' manes as headdresses and
were known to be very fierce. The Italians got so scared!
With no horses and many soldiers without weapons, their neat
retreat turned into a big, messy run for safety.

A Nation Celebrates

The night of March 1st was full of joy in the Ethiopian camp. Bright bonfires lit up the dark sky, and everyone shared sweet tej, a special honey drink. Drums beat loudly as people danced and laughed together.

The soldiers told proud stories about their brave fight. Sometimes, they even fired their rifles into the air to celebrate!

By defeating the Italian army and sending them running away in a big panic, Ethiopia had won its freedom!

Punishment and Mercy

After the battle, about 1,500 Askari, African soldiers who fought for the Italians, were captured. Menelik and the other leaders talked about what to do with them. It was decided they should be punished, and they were.

About 1,900 Italian soldiers were also captured. They walked a long way with the Ethiopian forces, more than 350 miles, all the way to Addis Ababa. It took more than two and a half months! When they got there, the city was filled with music and happy celebrations. The royal court had a big feast, and even the prisoners were invited! Pictures of Menelik and Taytu were hung proudly as musicians played, and everyone, friends and former enemies, shared food together.

To honor his victory, Empress Taytu followed a special tradition and put an earring on Emperor Menelik's ear.

The Vatican tried to help free Italy's young prisoners, and even Pope Leo XIII wrote to Emperor Menelik. But what really touched Menelik was a letter from a mother, written to her son Antonio, a prisoner in Ethiopia. She told of how she lit a candle and prayed for him. When Menelik read the letter, he said, "Your mother is a holy lady. Her prayers should be answered." He gave Antonio money and a mule and sent him home safely.

A Nation Stands Free

Finally, Emperor Menelik and Italy agreed to free all the prisoners. Italy promised to pay for all the costs of taking care of them. The agreement said that the prisoners "had been treated with the greatest care by His Majesty the Emperor of Ethiopia."

Ethiopia had won, and its independence was safe!

እሑድ	ሰኞ	ማክሰኞ	ረቡዕ	ሐሙስ	ዓርብ	ቅዳሜ
		፩	፪	፫	፬	፭
፮	፯	፰	፱	፲	፲፩	፲፪
፲፫	፲፬	፲፭	፲፮	፲፯	፲፰	፲፱
፳	፳፩	፳፪	፳፫	፳፬	፳፭	፳፮
፳፯	፳፰	፳፱	፴			

Fun Facts

- In Italy, if someone acted bold and fancy, people once said, "Who does she think she is, Empress Taytu?"

- In 1897, Emperor Menelik was in a famous magazine, which was kind of like being on the cover of TIME today!

- A French store and a German company made trading cards with pictures of Menelik and Taytu, just like baseball cards!

- After the Battle of Adwa, churches in America added names such as "Abyssinian" and "Ethiopian" to show love for Ethiopia. One of the most famous is the Abyssinian Baptist Church in Harlem, New York!

- For Queen Margherita of Italy's birthday, Menelik let 50 prisoners go free! He let 50 more go for the Russian king's big party!

- Even the pope was impressed! The Vatican said Menelik was one of the most important leaders in the world.

- People around the world were so amazed by Ethiopia's victory that some even wrote letters from faraway places such as Australia and New Zealand, asking, "Can we come be your soldiers?"

Can we join your army?

- Many African countries picked green, yellow, and red for their flags to honor Ethiopia's brave fight for freedom!

Glossary

- Abyssinia – An old name for Ethiopia, used in many historical texts.

- Amharic – The official language of Ethiopia. It comes from an ancient language called Ge'ez.

- Fitawrari - A traditional Ethiopian military hierarchy; translates to "commander of the vanguard or advance guard."

- Injera – A soft, spongy flatbread made from teff flour. It looks like a big pancake.

- Ras – A powerful Ethiopian title, similar to a duke. Rulers of large regions were often called "Ras."

- Tabot - A replica of the Ark of the Covenant.

- Tej - Ethiopian wine made from honey.

Bibliography

- Adwa: An African Victory. Produced and directed by Haile Gerima. NegodGwad Production Films.

- Assefa, Eshete. The Generals Who Lost [Amharic]. YouTube, uploaded by Sheger FM 102.1 Radio, 03 March 2023, https://www.youtube.com/watch?v=If0bELmxx6w&t=311s

- Assefa, Eshete. Adwa Documentary [Amharic]. YouTube, uploaded by Sheger FM 102.1 Radio, 03 March 2023, https://www.youtube.com/watch?v=sXdtR6vcP5U&t=2878s

- "The Battle of Adwa." Wikipedia, The Free Encyclopedia, Wikimedia Foundation, 17 May 2025, https://en.wikipedia.org/wiki/Battle_of_Adwa

- "Flags of Ethiopia." Wikipedia, The Free Encyclopedia, Wikimedia Foundation, 17 May 2025, https://en.wikipedia.org/wiki/Flag_of_Ethiopia

- Gnogno, Paulos. Dagmawi Atse Minelik [Emperor Menelik II]. Percy Brothers Limited, The Hotspurs Press, 1990.

- Jonas, Raymond. The Battle of Adwa: African Victory in the Age of Empire. The Belknap Press of Harvard University Press, 2011.

- McLachlan, Sean. Armies of the Adowa Campaign 1896: The Italian Disaster in Ethiopia. Osprey Publishing, 2011.

- "Taytu Betul: The Bad Cop Empress of Ethiopia." Rejected Princesses, 17 May 2025, https://www.rejectedprincesses.com/princesses/taytu-betul

www.ingramcontent.com/pod-product-compliance
Lightning Source LLC
Chambersburg PA
CBRC090829120626
46547CB00008B/633